MEL BAY'S GETTING INTO...... ACCORDION
by GARY DAHL

W9-BGN-325

CD CONTENTS

1. Intro
2. Treble Keyboard
3. Bass Keyboard
4. Left Hand Exercises
5. Review Coordination
6. Three Chord Song
7. More Treble Notes
8. Bass Solo Warm-ups
9. German Folk Song
10. Waltz
11. Polka
12. Alternating Basses
13. Eighth Note Counting Theory
14. Scale Technique
15. Whole & Half Steps, ♯'s, ♭'s, ♮'s
16. Stranger in Paradise
17. Scale Technique
18. Practice Daily
19. Rockin' the Blues
20. Come Back to Sorrento
21. Closer

1 2 3 4 5 6 7 8 9 0

Visit us on the Web at www.melbay.com — E-mail us at email@melbay.com

Contents

Foreword

The **Getting Into Accordion Method** follows the **First Lessons Book**. Most of today's accordionists are recreational players that took lessons during their school age years and now upon returning to the accordion need an adult oriented book that will teach and motivate the additional skills needed to become an advanced accordionist with the skills to learn and enjoy any style of music. This book presents very high level arrangements of favorite songs, including technique building exercises and beginning chord memorization. The **Getting Into Accordion Method** fills an important pedagogical niche that provides a structured program to assure step-by-step development. Together with additional selected solo arrangements, the **Chord Melody Method Book** and the **Scale Book with Jazz Scale Studies** will be sufficient material to guide the student from the beginner level to the professional level. Correspondence lessons with the author are strongly suggested to be successful with all of the books.

Gary Dahl

the new 'garydahl jazz/continental model'
(featuring a new 5 1/3 quint piccolo)

A Brief Guide to Slow Practice

By Gary Dahl

I decided when I started teaching thirty-seven years ago, each student would be required to demonstrate **slow practice tempos** in selected sections of a piece assigned a week earlier. At first, these tempos are rather like slow-motion and gradually increase only when the skill level is ready. I have never regretted this decision because it has produced many confident, satisfied accordionists.

What are the benefits of this kind of practicing?

- The student actually learns the piece faster, having had time to read the correct notes, time values, dynamics, etc.

- Performance slips are greatly reduced (a slip is not a mistake). A mistake is playing the same wrong notes at every performance, while an occasional slip sometimes just happens.

- Slow practice eliminates practice mistakes. Why should we practice a mistake? Not too logical is it?

- Control, especially in fast rhythmic pieces is much more secure. This is especially true in long scale-like passages.

- Because dynamics are exaggerated during slow practice, they retain their color at tempo.

- Slow practice and repetitions of short passages is essential to increase learning speed and to eliminate mistakes.

There are many more points I could list but these are the basics. Occasionally my students think I am some sort of Psychic because I can tell immediately if they have not done their slow practice. If it is a fairly new piece, the fingers are searching everywhere for the notes. Slow practice will enable you to learn quickly while fast practice will produce very slow results or none at all. Slow practice is not particularly fun but it is part of the discipline we must observe. I tell my students I am not asking them to slow practice because it is fun, in fact it can be boring. You have to bleed a little, pay the price to realize the exciting benefits. You can't learn in your sleep.

To the Adult Student: Music is for all to enjoy, both for listening pleasure and the thrill of playing the accordion confidently and musically. Music is a way of expressing ourselves. Many people would give anything to play an instrument with authority. Don't let your age get you down. It is literally true; you are never too old to learn. Many adults are happier now and getting more out of life by learning music.

Adult students will learn more at lessons using these suggestions:

- Make believe you are 10 years old again. Forget pre-conceived ideas.

- Don't talk too much–concentrate on listening.

- Let the teacher lead with the best sequence for you to reach your particular goals.

- Don't let your ego get in the way, even if you are an experienced player.

- Study harmony to dramatically enhance your current skills. You will then be able to produce your own arrangements–this is where the real fun is!

- Don't try to pick pieces way beyond your capability. It is always better to play a less difficult piece well than a more advanced selection sloppy; just experience the pleasure of high–quality music–making!

Popular Music in Today's Society

By Gary Dahl

Today's popular music is a group of various styles ... jazz, swing, country, blues, rock, cajun, zydeco, and others. The accordionist of today must gather together the knowledge of the melodic and harmonic flow of music to play in various genres and improvise/arrange skillfully. One cannot simply sit down to improvise successfully over 12–bar blues without having first studied how; similarly one cannot simply play a Beethoven sonata without first having studied how to play Beethoven.

What is needed, then, to accomplish professional-level playing in various genres? The answer is a thorough knowledge of harmony, chord structure, rhythm, and melody (including melodic improvisation) will provide useful training toward this goal. Along with this every accordionist needs to remember the basic rule of switch selection: use good taste appropriate to the style in which you are playing. Play polkas with a dry switch, play jazz with the bassoon switch, use musette tuned middle reeds for French musette, etc. (don't mix wet middle reeds with the bassoon and/or piccolo reeds because it irritates the non accordion public and also just sounds horrible...this is similar to an orchestra badly out of tune).

To play popular music skillfully one needs to use all the aforementioned skills together to develop a good playing technique. Once that has been accomplished tricky passages will be easier and open chords can be smoothly executed even in awkward positions. A popular accordionist in most cases can certainly play Dizzy Fingers etc.; this develops good technical skills which are applicable to any style. I know of several accordion soloists who perform primarily from music arranged by others. These same soloists would dearly love to be able to read lead sheets and improvise appropriately

A fully accomplished accordionist, possessing all the previously mentioned skills, can take a seemingly simple tune and play it with symphonic sophistication. Having this ability is similar to comparing skills required for kindergarten arithmetic to the skills required for a doctorate in mathematics! It raises the accordionist to an entirely new level. Why did Mozart, who could compose new melodies at will, write several variations on his older melodies? Why does a competent accordionist write, arrange, and improvise? A drawing from a child, while possessing artistic qualities, lacks the development and refinement of a trained visual artist.

The first place to begin is listening; all of the great musicians of the world listened to music with an attentive ear. Listen closely for the movement of harmony and the way instruments are used in an arrangement. Listen also to the variety of tempos and rhythms, keeping in mind that tempo refers only to speed and rhythm refers to the organization of notes. The accordion is a very sophisticated instrument, encompassing the equivalent of a melodic instrument (right-hand keyboard) with it's own backup combo (left-hand keyboard).

Everything present in music today has evolved from something previous–new styles have their own idiosyncrasies which must be learned individually (jazz, rock, cajun, polka, etc,) and they all depend on the same core elements; functional harmony, rhythm and melody. Every style is accessible if one only has a grasp of those central elements. Remember, merely buying paints and brushes doesn't make one the next Rembrandt; similarly, merely buying an accordion doesn't make one the next great accordionist.

The *Accordion is a Free Reed Instrument

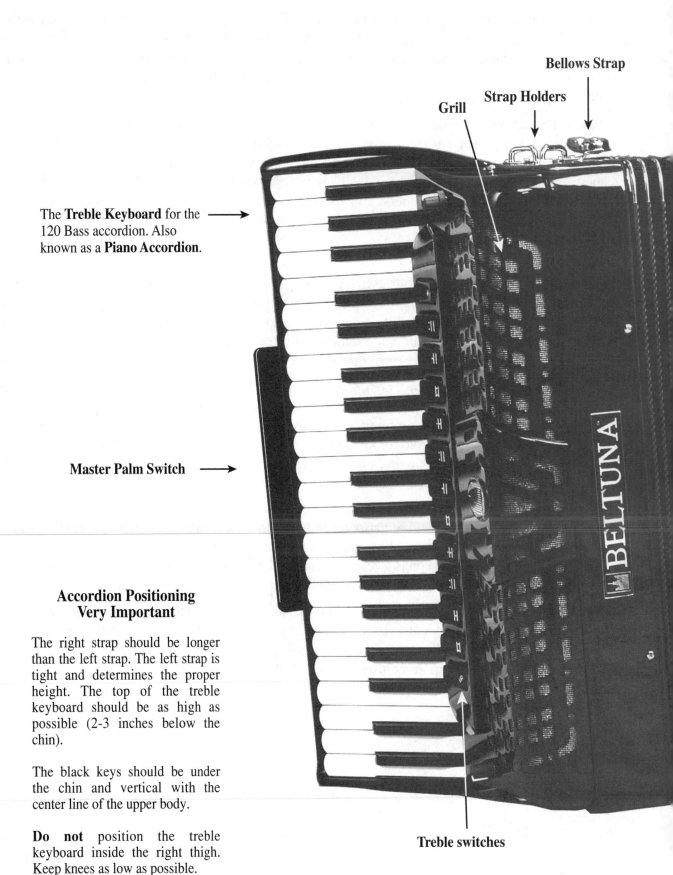

Bellows Strap

Strap Holders

Grill

The **Treble Keyboard** for the 120 Bass accordion. Also known as a **Piano Accordion**. →

Master Palm Switch →

Accordion Positioning
Very Important

The right strap should be longer than the left strap. The left strap is tight and determines the proper height. The top of the treble keyboard should be as high as possible (2-3 inches below the chin).

The black keys should be under the chin and vertical with the center line of the upper body.

Do not position the treble keyboard inside the right thigh. Keep knees as low as possible.

Treble switches

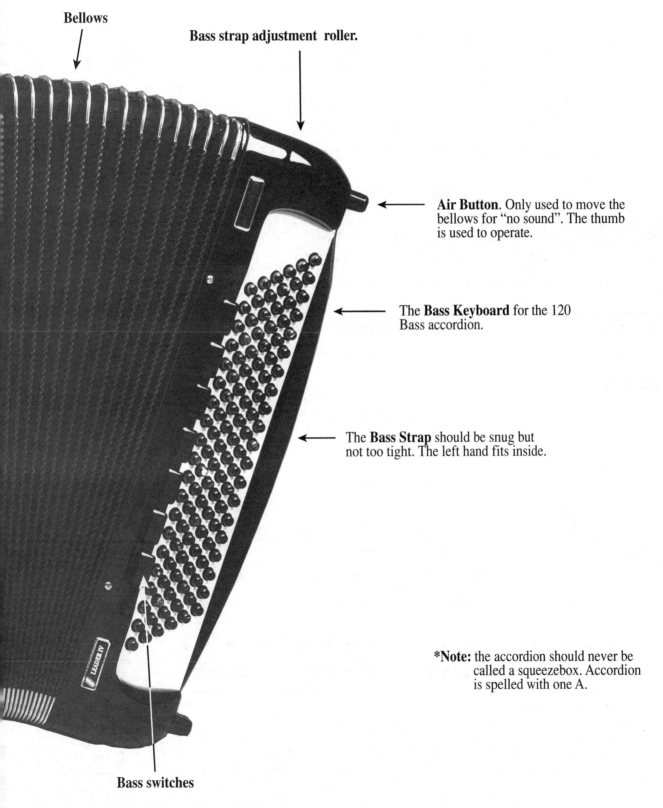

Bellows

Bass strap adjustment roller.

Air Button. Only used to move the bellows for "no sound". The thumb is used to operate.

The **Bass Keyboard** for the 120 Bass accordion.

The **Bass Strap** should be snug but not too tight. The left hand fits inside.

*Note: the accordion should never be called a squeezebox. Accordion is spelled with one A.

Bass switches

Unlock the **Bottom Bellows Strap** before putting on the accordion in sitting position.

Review Basic Theory

This is a **Staff**. It has 5 lines and 4 spaces as numbered.

This is a **Treble Clef Sign**. Adding this sign changes the name to **Treble Staff**.
The bottom line is always E. The bottom space is F.

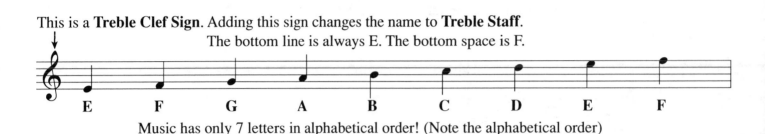

E   F   G   A   B   C   D   E   F

Music has only 7 letters in alphabetical order! (Note the alphabetical order)

Types of Notes

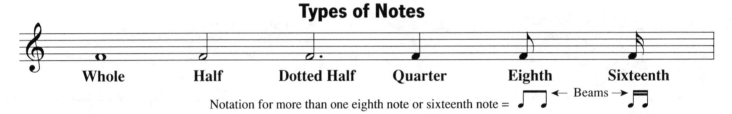

Whole   **Half**   **Dotted Half**   **Quarter**   **Eighth**   **Sixteenth**

Notation for more than one eighth note or sixteenth note =   ← Beams →

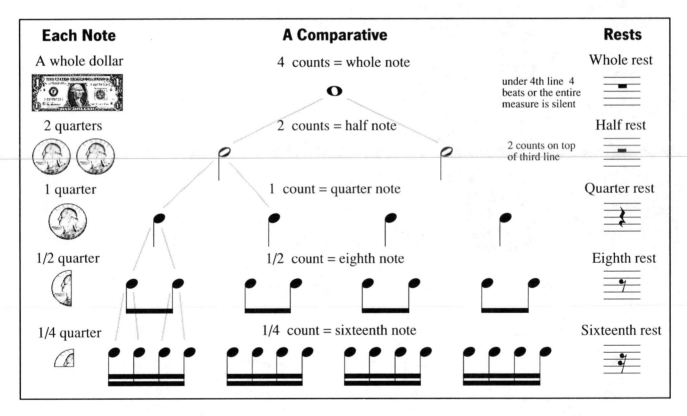

Each Note	A Comparative	Rests
A whole dollar	4 counts = whole note	Whole rest
		under 4th line 4 beats or the entire measure is silent
2 quarters	2 counts = half note	Half rest
		2 counts on top of third line
1 quarter	1 count = quarter note	Quarter rest
1/2 quarter	1/2 count = eighth note	Eighth rest
1/4 quarter	1/4 count = sixteenth note	Sixteenth rest

2 numbers at the beginning is a **Time Signature**. It officially tells us how to count time. The top number is *counts per measure*. The bottom 4 represents the quarter note, (as in 4 quarters in a dollar) and officially gives the quarter note one count.

Double bar line (End of Song)

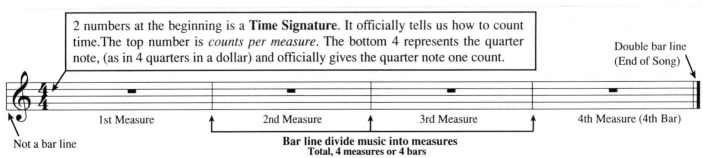

1st Measure   2nd Measure   3rd Measure   4th Measure (4th Bar)

Not a bar line

Bar line divide music into measures
Total, 4 measures or 4 bars

Review Important Music Signs

Music Signs

⟨⟨ *Crescendo (cresc.)* = Gradually louder.

\> Accent   ∧ Stronger Accent

⟩⟩ *Diminuendo (dim.)* = Gradually softer.

The *Staccato* sign (a dot over a note) = play half value. Play these crisply and short.

The *Tenuto* sign = hold for full value.

The *Fermata* = hold the note twice the written value or more if desired.

𝄋 The *"Sign"* = repeat from this sign *(al segno)*.

⊕ The *Coda* sign = play ⊕ to ⊕ after a repeat.

⅟. = Repeat previous measure.

tr *Trill* = two notes alternating rapidly using the next scale tone higher unless notated differently.

tr = ▦
Trill for 1 count

Glissando = slide from note to note.

× = Double sharp.

♭♭ = Double flat.

♪ = Short grace note *(acciaccatura)*.
Play extremely quickly before the prime note... Almost at the same time slur into prime.

Tempo
(Playing Speed, Rate of Speed)

Largo = Slowly (10 MPH).

Larghetto = Less slowly (15 MPH).

Adagio = Slower than **Andante** (20 MPH).

Andante = Slowly but moving (30 MPH).

Moderato = In moderate speed (40–50 MPH).

Allegretto = Lively, slower than **Allegro** (60 MPH).

Allegro = Fast (70 MPH).

Vivace = *Vivo,* faster than **Allegro** (80 MPH).

Presto = Rapidly (90 MPH).

Prestissimo = As fast as possible (100 MPH).

rit. (ritardando) = Gradually slowing down.

accel. (accelerando) = Gradually faster.

poco a poco = Little by little.

Dynamic Signs
(Expression* Signs)

p   *Piano* – Softly

pp   *Pianissimo* – Very softly

ppp *Pianississimo* – Softly as possible

f   *Forte* – Loud

ff   *Fortissimo* – Very loud

fff *Fortississimo* – Loud as possible

mf   *Mezzo forte* – Moderately loud

mp   *Mezzo piano* – Moderately soft

There are many more signs and words. I suggest purchasing the Mel Bay Music Dictionary for reference.

* **Expression:** that quality in a composition or performance which appeals to our feelings, taste or judgement displayed in rendering a composition and imparting to it the sentiment of the author.

Before We Begin Playing

Practice operating the bellows:

1. Place left hand inside the bass strap. Use the air button and push bellows in to close completely and hold in until playing.

2. Press on the R.H. ⊖ (Bassoon) or ⊕ (Bandoneon) or ⊙⊙ (Violin) switch.

3. Place left hand in the approximate middle of the side bass panel after closing the bellows before starting to pull out.

Note: The bellows must be pulled (out) and pushed (in) smoothly, not in a jerky fashion. Pulling out will open the bellows more at the top (fan like). Keep the elbow close to your side. As you pull out, the bellows will move downward a little automatically and to the back slightly. Don't worry, the bellows can bend. Simply retrace your steps upon pushing in. (Do **NOT** lift up your bellows while pushing in.)

Note: The middle of the accordion (botton of the bellows), will rest on top of the left thigh and the bellows will move to the left, outside and over the thigh. See Fig. C.

Fig. A
The easiest and preferred method to take your accordion out and back in the case. A quality case is designed to stay open in a V position without tipping.

Fig. B
Correct standing position.

Fig. C
Correct sitting position. (Note the black keys under the chin and vertical.)

Review Playing the Right Hand

and the Right Hand Position

Before playing our Right Hand (treble), we must discuss the hand position.

1. Keep your thumb level on the keyboard and parallel to the keys.

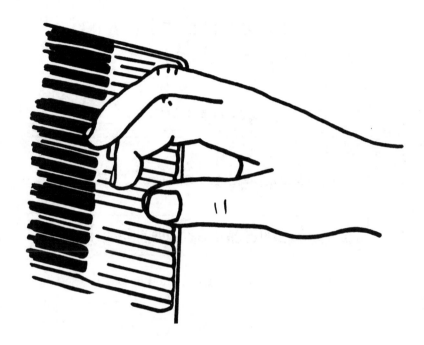

2. All other fingers should be slightly curved and close to the black keys, but not inside the black keys.

3. Keep your elbow out and back a little so your wrist is level and relaxed (and remember, short fingernails).

Review the Treble Keyboard
(Right Hand)

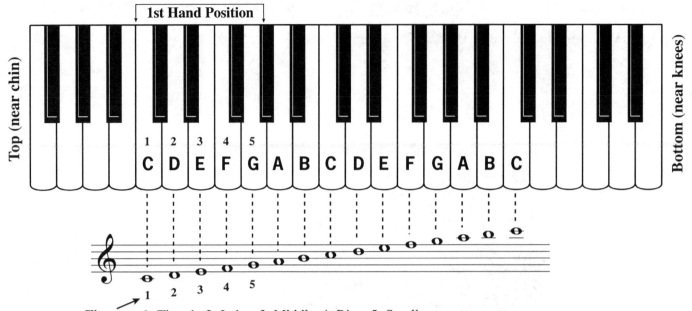

Top (near chin)   1st Hand Position   Bottom (near knees)

Fingers: 1=Thumb, 2=Index, 3=Middle, 4=Ring, 5=Small

 Keep eyes on music while playing

(Quickly review page 7 before playing R.H.)

Dotted half note: hold down 3 counts

Medium volume

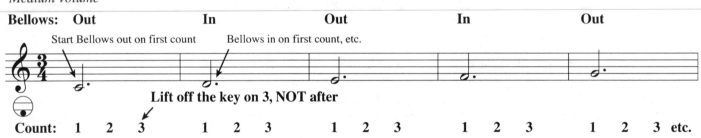

Bellows:	Out	In	Out	In	Out

Start Bellows out on first count   Bellows in on first count, etc.

Lift off the key on 3, NOT after

| Count: | 1 | 2 | 3 | 1 | 2 | 3 | 1 | 2 | 3 | 1 | 2 | 3 | 1 | 2 | 3 etc. |

Count Out Loud Press and hold the key down on one and **LIFT OFF** on three.

In	Out	In	Out	In

Practice daily until played from start to end without stopping.
Always keep constant bellows pressure while playing.

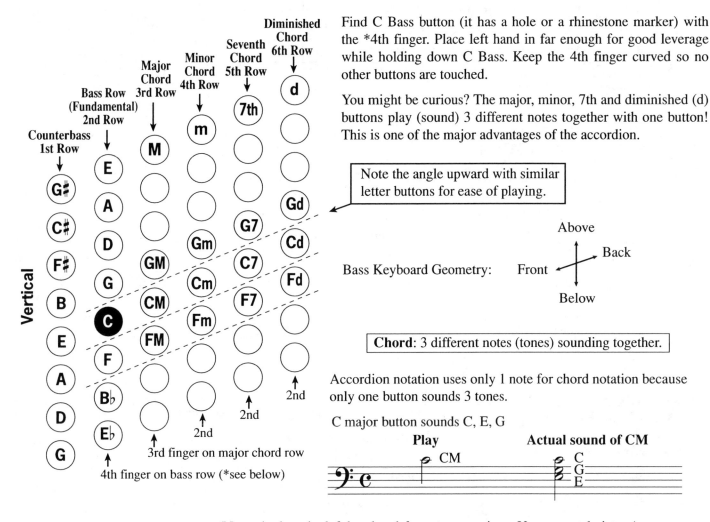

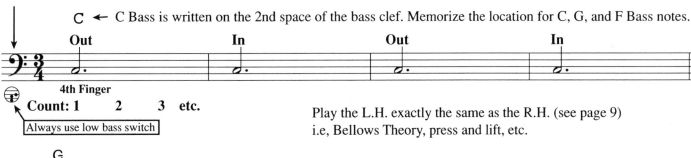

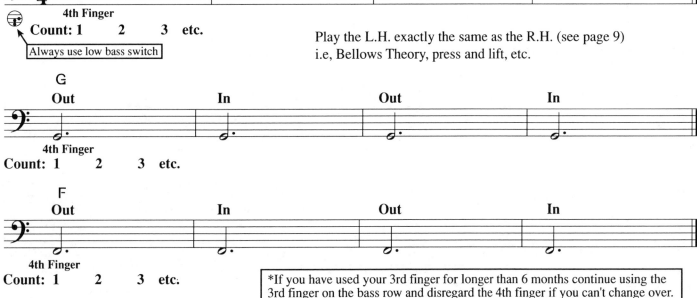

Reviewing the Left Hand (Bass Clef)

Find C Bass button (it has a hole or a rhinestone marker) with the *4th finger. Place left hand in far enough for good leverage while holding down C Bass. Keep the 4th finger curved so no other buttons are touched.

You might be curious? The major, minor, 7th and diminished (d) buttons play (sound) 3 different notes together with one button! This is one of the major advantages of the accordion.

Note the angle upward with similar letter buttons for ease of playing.

Bass Keyboard Geometry: Above / Back / Front / Below

Chord: 3 different notes (tones) sounding together.

Accordion notation uses only 1 note for chord notation because only one button sounds 3 tones.

C major button sounds C, E, G

Play — CM   Actual sound of CM — C, G, E

(Never look at the left hand and **do not** use a mirror. Use a mental picture)

This is a **Bass Clef Sign**. Play on the bass keyboard.

C ← C Bass is written on the 2nd space of the bass clef. Memorize the location for C, G, and F Bass notes.

4th Finger
Count: 1   2   3   etc.
Always use low bass switch

Play the L.H. exactly the same as the R.H. (see page 9)
i.e, Bellows Theory, press and lift, etc.

G
4th Finger
Count: 1   2   3   etc.

F
4th Finger
Count: 1   2   3   etc.

*If you have used your 3rd finger for longer than 6 months continue using the 3rd finger on the bass row and disregard the 4th finger if you can't change over.

13

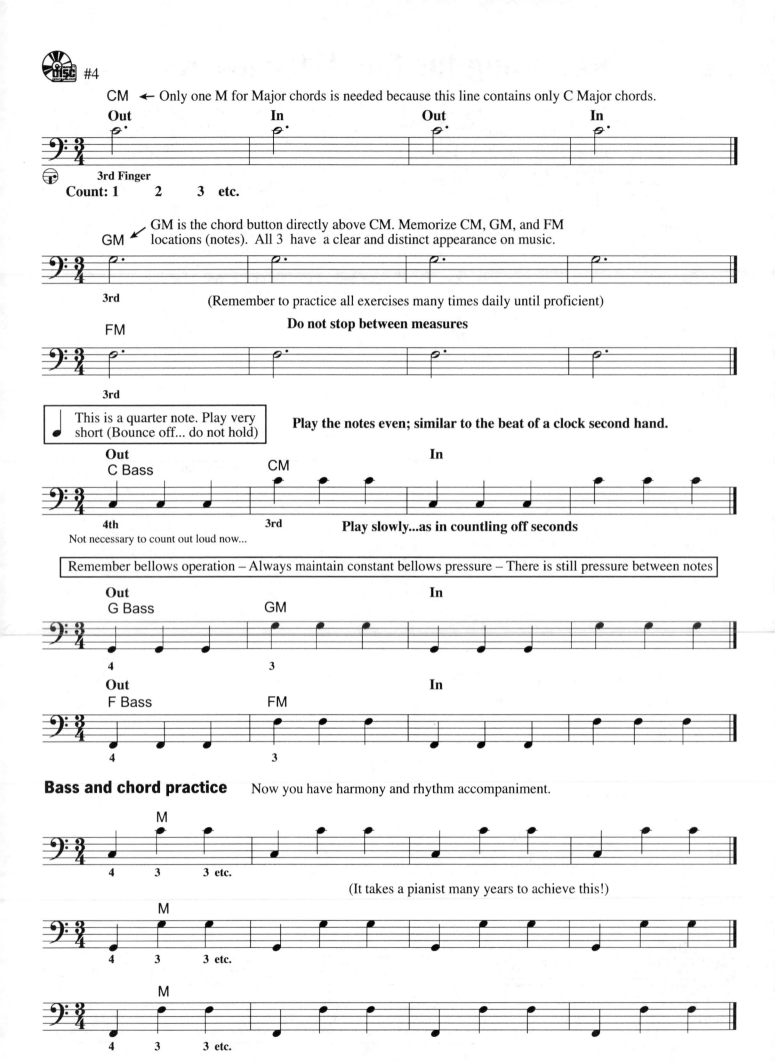

CM ← Only one M for Major chords is needed because this line contains only C Major chords.

Out **In** **Out** **In**

3rd Finger
Count: 1   2   3   etc.

GM is the chord button directly above CM. Memorize CM, GM, and FM
GM ↙ locations (notes). All 3 have a clear and distinct appearance on music.

3rd

(Remember to practice all exercises many times daily until proficient)

FM **Do not stop between measures**

3rd

This is a quarter note. Play very short (Bounce off... do not hold) **Play the notes even; similar to the beat of a clock second hand.**

Out   **In**
C Bass   CM

4th   3rd   **Play slowly...as in countling off seconds**
Not necessary to count out loud now...

Remember bellows operation – Always maintain constant bellows pressure – There is still pressure between notes

Out   **In**
G Bass   GM

4   3

Out   **In**
F Bass   FM

4   3

Bass and chord practice   Now you have harmony and rhythm accompaniment.

M

4   3   3 etc.

(It takes a pianist many years to achieve this!)

M

4   3   3 etc.

M

4   3   3 etc.

14

Review 𝄞 and 𝄢 Together

Review Coordination

1. Start both hands at the same time (1st count).
2. Hold R.H. for 3 counts and lift off on the 3rd count.

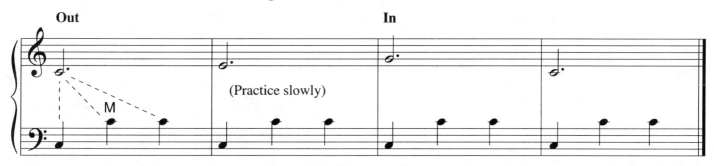

Do not continue until this line can be played without stopping

Remember to play short

Lift off the right hand in the 3rd count of the L.H. chord

(Practice slowly)

Say the name of each note out loud (Review treble keyboard chart)

C   D   E   G   F   E   F   E   D   E   D   C

Random note selection (no melody)

| ♩ Quarter note = one count |
| play short; same as L.H. |

Say the name of the note out loud while playing. Do not write names under each note.

#6

A Three Chord Song
(C Major, G Major, F Major)

Italian for moderately

Moderato (medium speed)

Only the starting finger is necessary to establish the hand position on the treble keyboard. At this time, use your note reading ability.

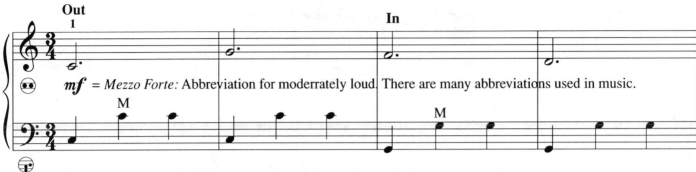

mf = *Mezzo Forte:* Abbreviation for moderrately loud. There are many abbreviations used in music.

Italian is considered the universal language for music.

Never change bellows direction while holding a note. Change direction on a new note.

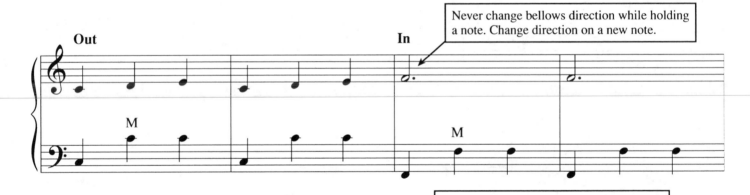

This is a **tie**. Ties connect similar position notes. Hold down until the final count. Do not change Bellows direction.

Do not lift off of this note

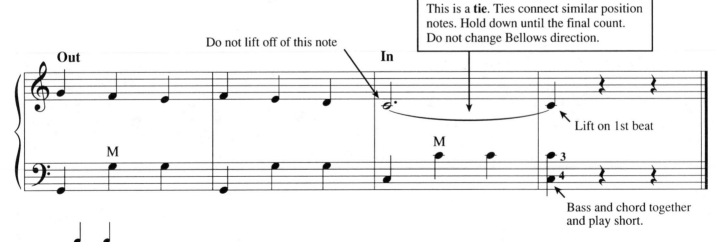

Lift on 1st beat

Bass and chord together and play short.

Ties will be written under or over the notes as determined by the best notation procedures.

16

Reviewing More Treble Notes
(So we can play more interesting songs!)

Top (chin)

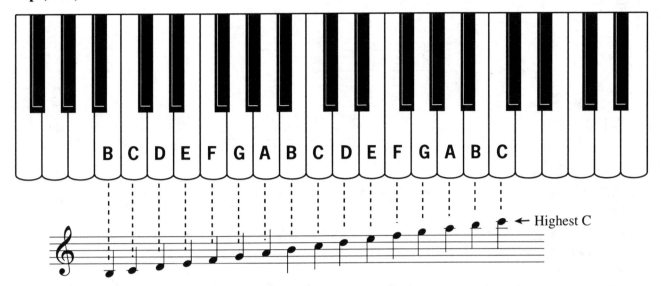

This isn't as hard as it looks....Just memorize. It will be simple after repetitive practice.

← The added short lines above and below the staff are **Ledger Lines**.

Why we need Ledger Lines is obvious.

4 counts per measure

Fingering is always logical...common sense

Cross 2nd finger over...very easy...Do Not play inside the black keys!

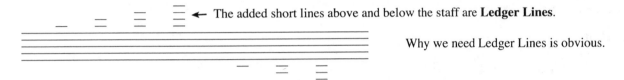

Very important: say each letter name out loud while playing each note. Do not write in letter names of each note.

Change fingers on the same key to raise our hand position.

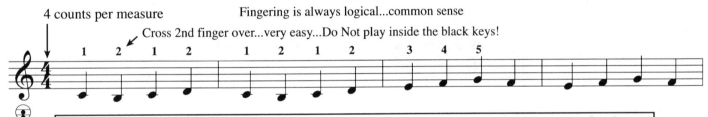

(You can't practice this note reading exercise too much!)

Play this exercise 2 ways: **short,** tap each key (note), and **legato,** hold down each note until the next note is played

More legato hints: strike each key....similar to a hammer hitting a nail.

Bring thumb up to B.
This will establish a new hand position

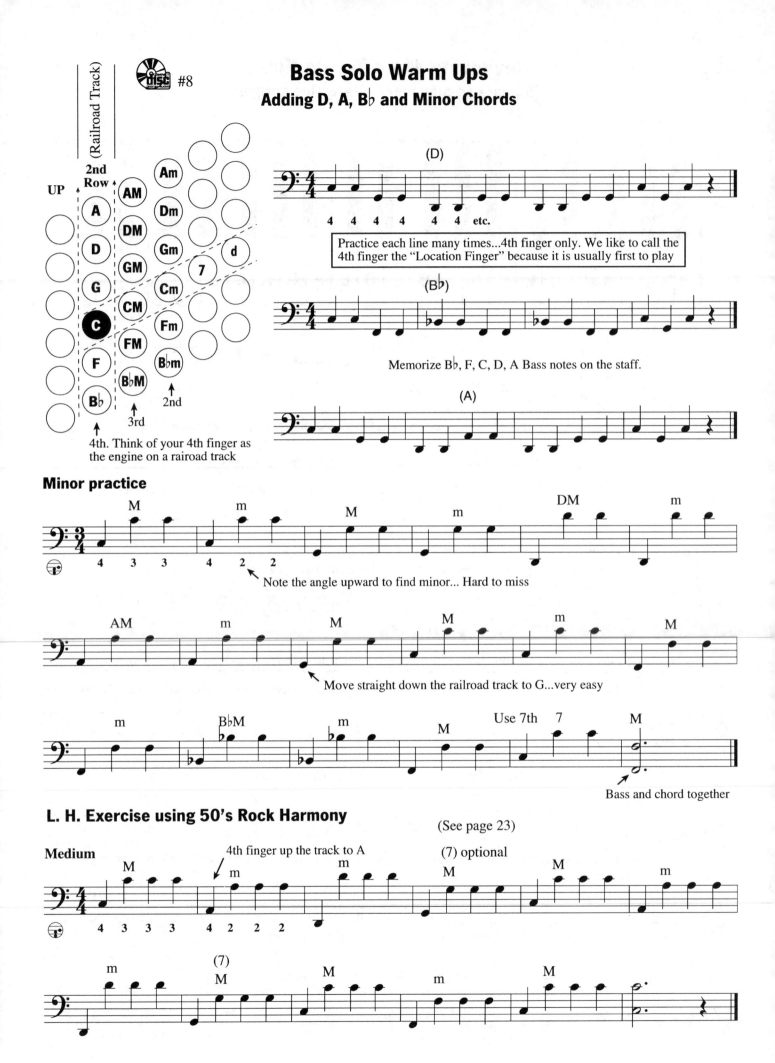

Bass Solo Warm Ups
Adding D, A, B♭ and Minor Chords

#8

Practice each line many times...4th finger only. We like to call the 4th finger the "Location Finger" because it is usually first to play

Memorize B♭, F, C, D, A Bass notes on the staff.

(Railroad Track)

UP

2nd Row

4th. Think of your 4th finger as the engine on a railroad track

Minor practice

Note the angle upward to find minor... Hard to miss

Move straight down the railroad track to G...very easy

Bass and chord together

Use 7th

L. H. Exercise using 50's Rock Harmony

(See page 23)

Medium

4th finger up the track to A

(7) optional

18

Du, Du Liegst Mir Im Herzen

German Folk Song

19

Slurs

*Slurs connect unlike notes.   The **Slur**: hold the note until the next is played. Do not lift off before the next note is played.

> To Slur similar notes: hold note as long as possible and quickly move up and down for the next similar note on the proper beat. The finger will most likely not lift off the key. Learn to feel the spring loaded key.

First and Second Ending

1. (First time only)   2. (Second time only)

Always repeat back to the nearest sign facing. Do this once.

Under and Over

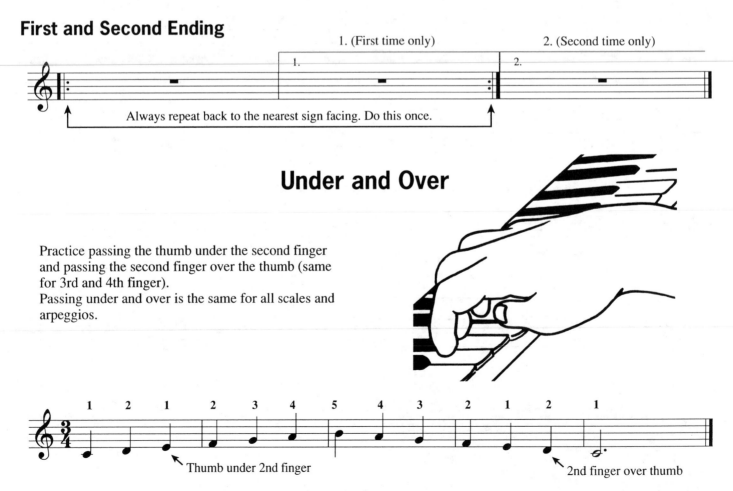

Practice passing the thumb under the second finger and passing the second finger over the thumb (same for 3rd and 4th finger).
Passing under and over is the same for all scales and arpeggios.

Thumb under 2nd finger   2nd finger over thumb

Waltz

Von Suppe

Review the Alternating Basses

... to provide a more interesting and harmonically correct background for the R. H. melody.

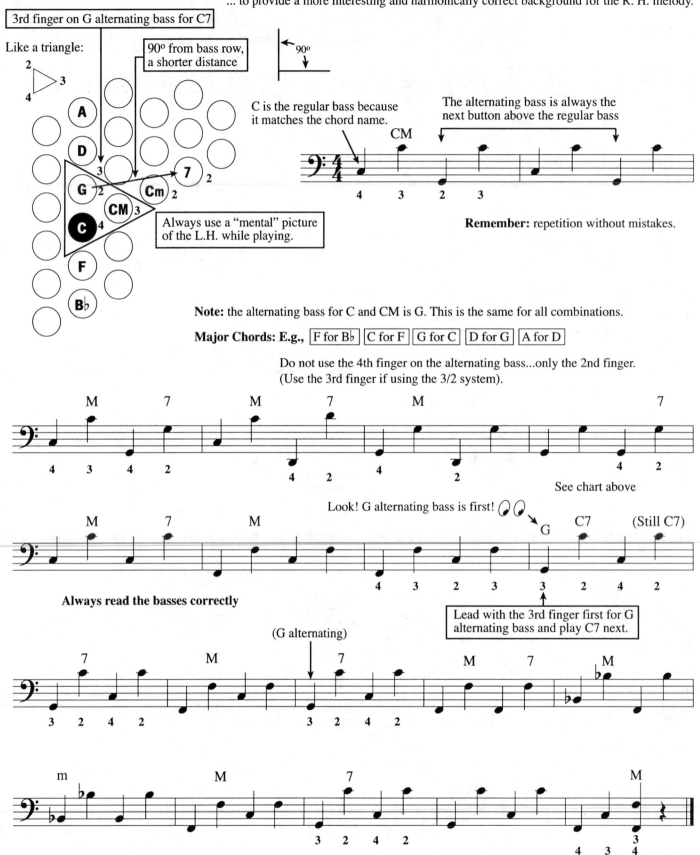

3rd finger on G alternating bass for C7

Like a triangle:

90° from bass row, a shorter distance

90°

C is the regular bass because it matches the chord name.

The alternating bass is always the next button above the regular bass

Always use a "mental" picture of the L.H. while playing.

Remember: repetition without mistakes.

Note: the alternating bass for C and CM is G. This is the same for all combinations.

Major Chords: E.g., F for B♭ · C for F · G for C · D for G · A for D

Do not use the 4th finger on the alternating bass...only the 2nd finger.
(Use the 3rd finger if using the 3/2 system).

See chart above

Look! G alternating bass is first!

Always read the basses correctly

Lead with the 3rd finger first for G alternating bass and play C7 next.

(G alternating)

22

The Village Tavern Polka
Reviewing the L.H. 7th chord

Practice:

Repeat until on automatic!

Play this line 20 times daily

Important! Remember: practice slowly enough for **NO** mistakes while in repetition.

Allegretto (lively, not too fast)

f *Forte* – loud

First four measures is the **Intro**

All ♩ notes short.

Remember: play all ♩ notes short.

Most of the time the alternating bass is **FIRST** for 7th chord

Do not write in letter names of notes

Stretch in front of C

Reviewing Eighth Notes
And Counting Theory

Flag

Eighth notes look like this when only one flag is required.

Beam
Two or more will connect with a beam

3

= 2 eighth notes = 1 quarter note

𝄾 ← This is an Eighth Rest

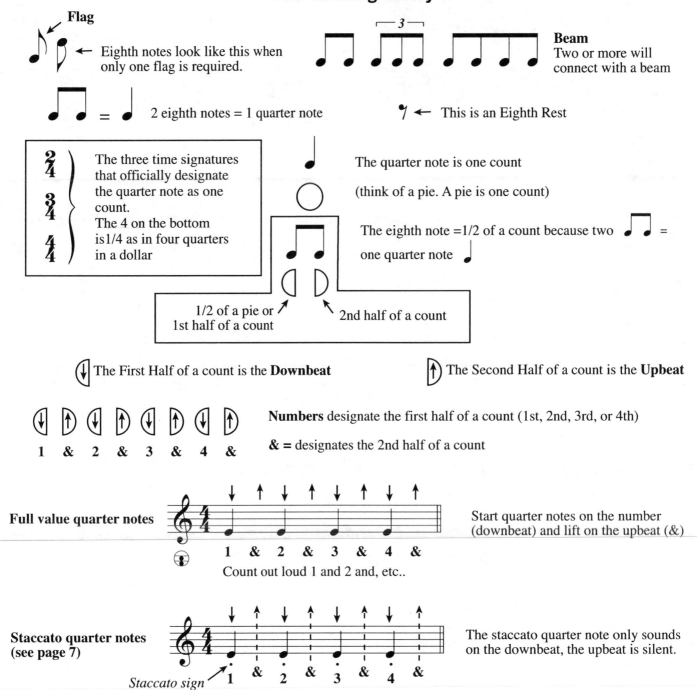

2/4
3/4
4/4
} The three time signatures that officially designate the quarter note as one count.
The 4 on the bottom is 1/4 as in four quarters in a dollar

The quarter note is one count

(think of a pie. A pie is one count)

The eighth note =1/2 of a count because two = one quarter note

1/2 of a pie or 1st half of a count ↗   ↖ 2nd half of a count

The First Half of a count is the **Downbeat**

The Second Half of a count is the **Upbeat**

1 & 2 & 3 & 4 &

Numbers designate the first half of a count (1st, 2nd, 3rd, or 4th)

& = designates the 2nd half of a count

Full value quarter notes

1 & 2 & 3 & 4 &

Count out loud 1 and 2 and, etc..

Start quarter notes on the number (downbeat) and lift on the upbeat (&)

Staccato quarter notes (see page 7)

Staccato sign ↗ 1 & 2 & 3 & 4 &

The staccato quarter note only sounds on the downbeat, the upbeat is silent.

Note: music for faster tempos are usually written in 2/4 for accurate interpretation.

Correct Bass and chord is automatically short

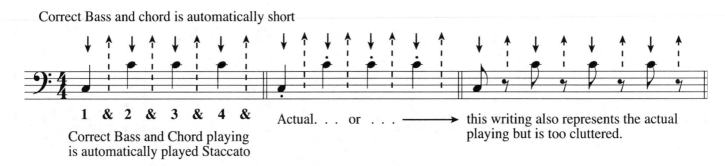

1 & 2 & 3 & 4 &

Correct Bass and Chord playing is automatically played Staccato

Actual. . . or . . . ⟶ this writing also represents the actual playing but is too cluttered.

24

Exercises

Slowly at first, then play at faster tempos.
Repeat daily until proficient

Remember: The downbeats (1, 2, 3, 4) must be steady and even.

(Staccato)

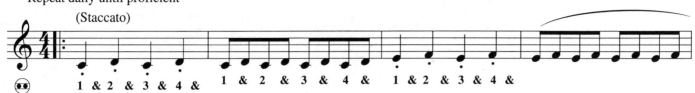

1 & 2 & 3 & 4 &   1 & 2 & 3 & 4 &   1 & 2 & 3 & 4 &

Count when playing slowly .... not possible at faster tempos

Legato = slur = connect notes smoothly

The Same Exercise, Both Hands

(Detached)

M

7   M   7   M

- Repeat 10 to 20 times daily

- Start slowly

- Practice with NO errors

- Gradually increase speed to your maximum but maintain an even rhythm.
(**Rhythm:** the organization of notes within a measure)

Reviewing the C Major Scale
(review page 21)

Practice at least 25 times daily

Practice staccato and legato. Start slowly and gradually increase speed.

thumb under the 3rd finger

3rd finger over the thumb

Note: Make sure your 3rd finger is fairly close to the black keys when crossing over
(tip of the thumb remains in approx. center of white keys) (see pg. 8)

C Major Scale Exercise
Gradually increase speed to your maximum but maintain an even rhythm

Staccato & Legato

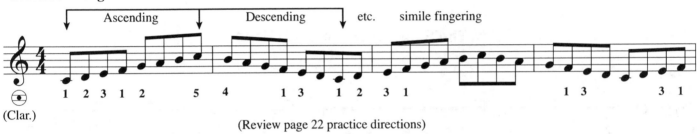

(Clar.)

(Review page 22 practice directions)

(Remember hand position and accordion positioning)

At this time the student should begin in-depth scale study using the Mel Bay *Master Accordion Scale Book with Jazz Scale Studies (MB99762)*.

Staccato & Legato

𝐂 = Common Time, same as **4/4**. ₵ = Usually faster tempo, 1st and 3rd beats similar to **2/4** time.

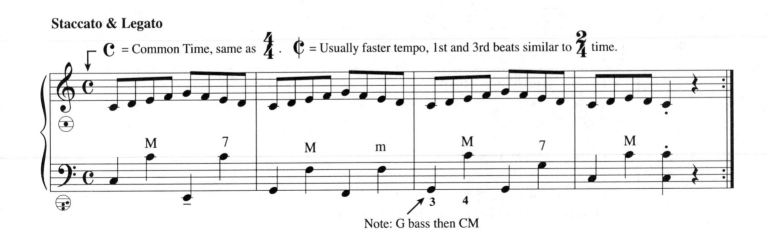

Note: G bass then CM

Review Half Steps, Whole Steps, Sharps (♯), Flats (♭), Naturals (♮)

(a very important page)

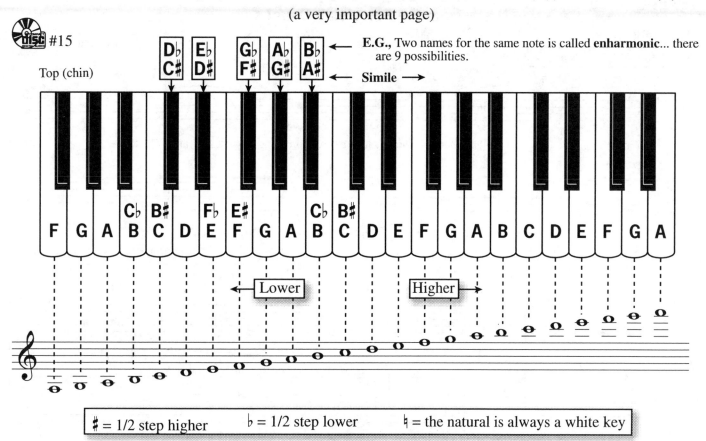

E.G., Two names for the same note is called **enharmonic**... there are 9 possibilities.

← **Simile** →

♯ = 1/2 step higher　　♭ = 1/2 step lower　　♮ = the natural is always a white key

The 1/2 step is the smallest interval from any treble key to the very next key. Say the following notes out loud and play at least once a day until proficient.

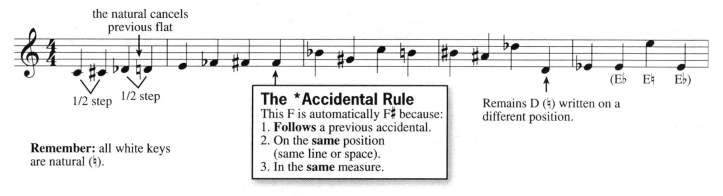

the natural cancels previous flat

1/2 step　　1/2 step

Remember: all white keys are natural (♮).

The *Accidental Rule
This F is automatically F♯ because:
1. **Follows** a previous accidental.
2. On the **same** position (same line or space).
3. In the **same** measure.

Remains D (♮) written on a different position.

(E♭　E♮　E♭)

Whole Steps Examples – Find on Keyboard

w, etc.

w, etc.

Memorize

All:　　C & D　　D & E　　G & A　　A & B are whole steps　　B & C　　E & F are always 1/2 steps

*Accidentals are any notes not occurring in the key signature. Accidentals are only effective in the measures in which they appear.

#16

Stranger in Paradise
from the Polovtsian Dances

Alexander Borodin

Moderato

Key of G, all F's are F♯

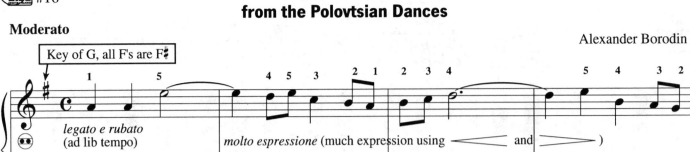

Chord only style, use same fingers on chords, use 4th for location

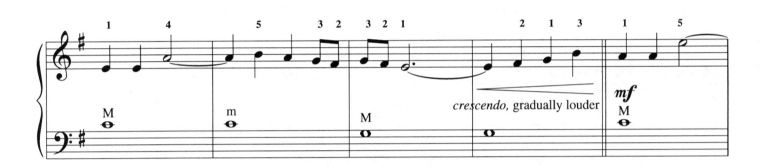

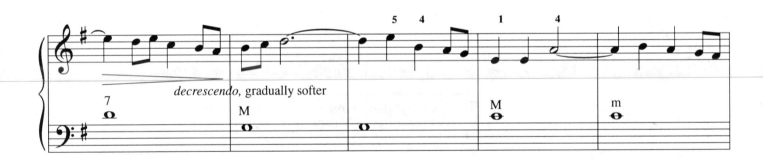

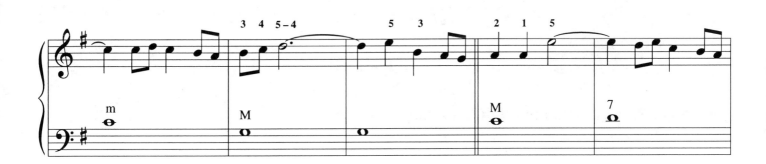

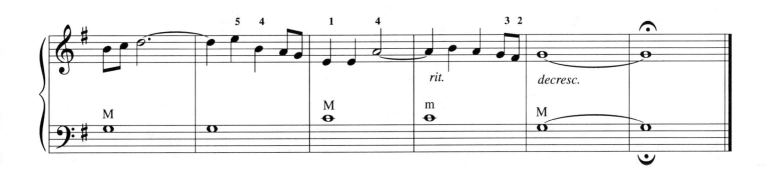

Key Signatures, 5 Major Scales – Daily Warm-ups

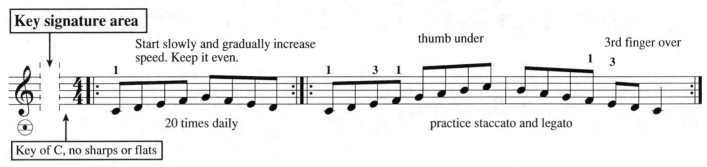

Key signature area

Start slowly and gradually increase speed. Keep it even.

thumb under

3rd finger over

20 times daily

practice staccato and legato

Key of C, no sharps or flats

Review Staccato: "Tap" the keys quickly and lightly; fingers and wrist only; similar to bouncing a basketball. Do not use the arm; stay relaxed.

Review Legato: Lift each finger and strike each key; similar to a hammer hitting a nail. The passing under with the thumb and crossing over with the 3rd or 4th finger is a little more difficult on a vertical keyboard. The following exercise will exaggerate the process for flexibility and control.

Stretching and bending... Do this exercise between each scale practice.

Legato only

Each 10 to 20 times daily.
Hint: Start with bellows closed and maintain steady medium pressure.

Ear training: Try to sing each scale note.

The Major Scale Whole Step Half Step Pattern

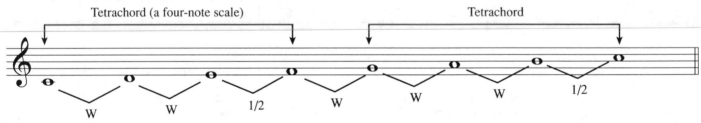

Tetrachord (a four-note scale)

Tetrachord

Key of G, all F's are sharp... anywhere on the staff

G Major Scale*

Repeat 10 times daily

Key of D, all F's and C's are sharp... any location on the staff

*For more practice use Mel Bay's *Master Accordion Scale Book (MB99762)*.

Practice All 10 Times Daily

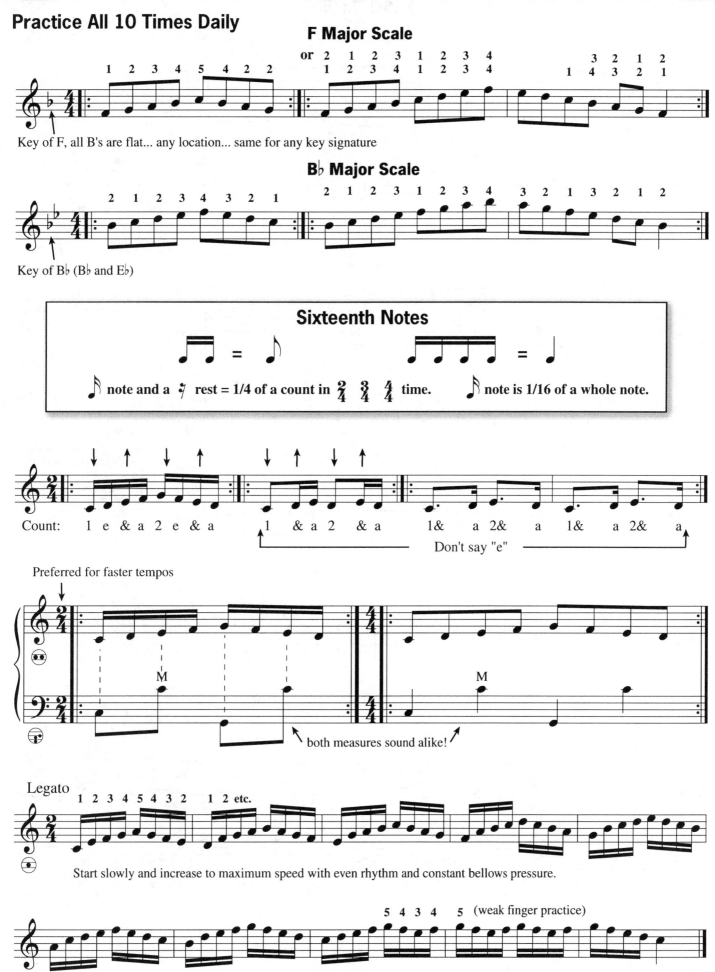

F Major Scale

Key of F, all B's are flat... any location... same for any key signature

B♭ Major Scale

Key of B♭ (B♭ and E♭)

Sixteenth Notes

♪ note and a 𝄽 rest = 1/4 of a count in 2/4 3/4 4/4 time.   ♪ note is 1/16 of a whole note.

Count: 1 e & a 2 e & a   1 & a 2 & a   1& a 2& a 1& a 2& a
Don't say "e"

Preferred for faster tempos

M   M

both measures sound alike!

Legato   1 2 3 4 5 4 3 2   1 2 etc.

Start slowly and increase to maximum speed with even rhythm and constant bellows pressure.

5 4 3 4   5 (weak finger practice)

Meadowlands
a study in ties

Moderato

V. Gussev

slide 4th

slide bass finger down
to E♭, there is 1/2
count available

— = *tenuto,* hold full value

rit. e decrescendo poco a poco

Start with bottom note
and hold each upward.

More Bass Patterns

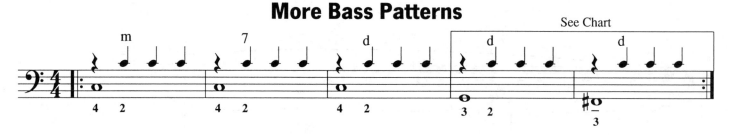

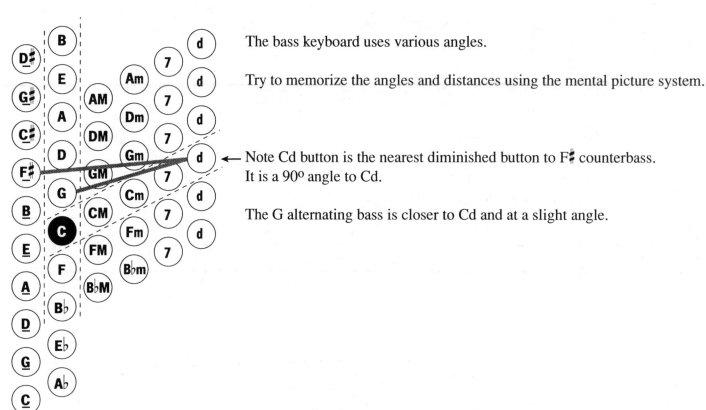

The bass keyboard uses various angles.

Try to memorize the angles and distances using the mental picture system.

← Note Cd button is the nearest diminished button to F♯ counterbass. It is a 90° angle to Cd.

The G alternating bass is closer to Cd and at a slight angle.

Always listen to the supporting L.H., also thought of as counterpoint... a counter supporting melody.

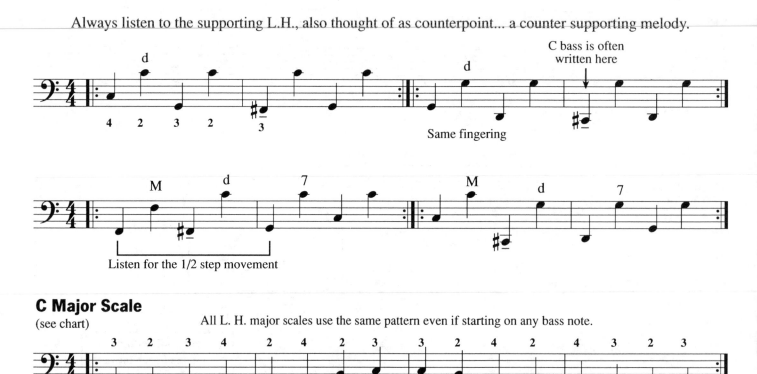

C Major Scale
(see chart)

All L. H. major scales use the same pattern even if starting on any bass note.

The Triplet

is equal to ♩ ♩ **or** ♩ **in time value**

Each note of a triplet is 1/3 of a count. Count: 1 & a, etc. We learn to "feel" 3 notes to one count.

20 times

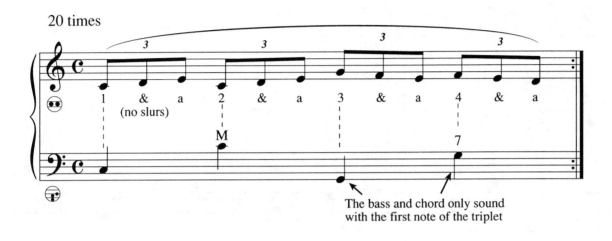

1 &a (no slurs) 2 &a 3 &a 4 &a

M 7

The bass and chord only sound with the first note of the triplet

20 times

1 2 M 7 M 2 5 7

4 5 4 4 7 M

Take Me Out to the Ball Game

Triads
an introduction to chord memorization
(for lead sheet and harmony applications)

There are 4 basic triads, chords composed of 3 different letter names (notes): major, minor, diminished and augmented. In popular music of the 70's to the present a variation of one of these is often heard. It is the suspended chord.

The following example shows all 5 types of triads.

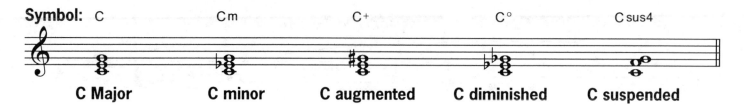

Chords are built from scales or intervals. The C major scale is an example.

Degrees of the major scale

The major triad = 1st, 3rd, 5th degrees of the major scale

Root positions are equally spaced (3 lines or 3 spaces). The bottom note of a chord in root position is the letter name of the chord

Cm = 1, ♭3, 5 of the major scale (flat the 3rd)

A 4-part chord has 4 positions.

C7 = 1, 3, 5, ♭7 of the major scale (flat the 7th). Full title: Dominant 7th

38

Beginning lead sheet practice: take your time . . . discipline and patience.

Practice inversions only to . . ."get the feel" of each chord.

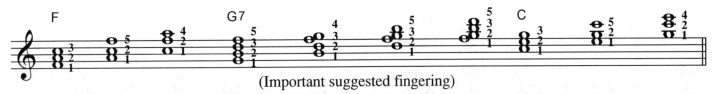

(Important suggested fingering)

C = Play C Major triad notes below each written melody note.

(Do not write in the harmony notes)

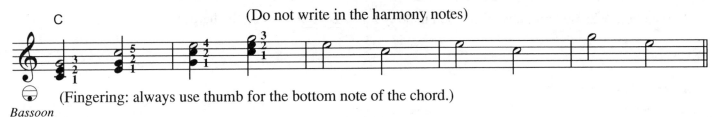

(Fingering: always use thumb for the bottom note of the chord.)

Bassoon

The first two measures include the harmony notes in black to get you started. The following measures require the correct harmony notes added using memory. Do not write in the harmony notes.

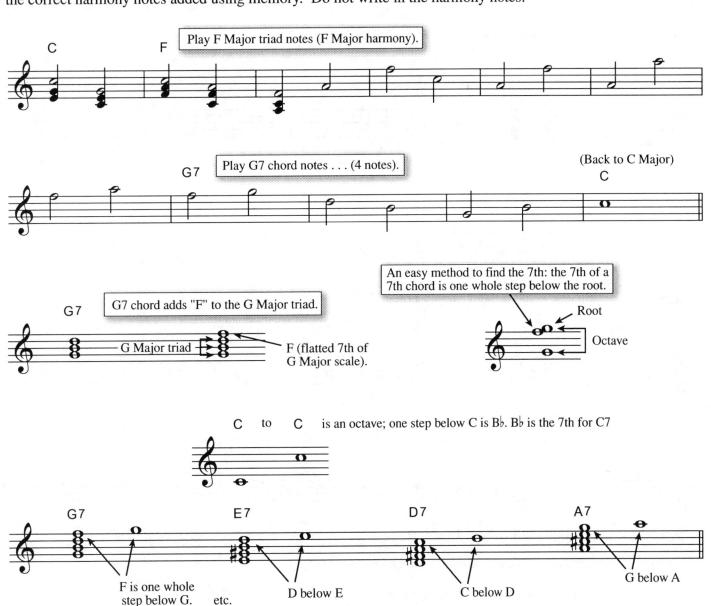

39

Practice the following chords with **all inversions** to prepare for exercise 1.

This is not memory work, only an introduction to each chord.

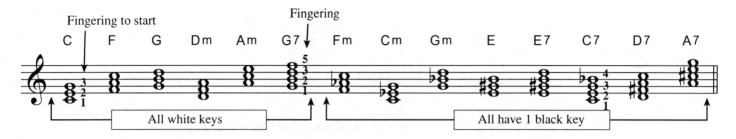

Remember: Add the harmony below each melody note. **Do <u>not</u>** write in the harmony.

Exercise 1

Black notes are added only to help the student in beginning stages.

Remember. . . do not write in the harmony notes.

Remember to use logical fingering. This exersice is learned when played Andante without stopping.

Always use the 3rd or 4th finger when the black key is on top.

For a complete education we recommend *Chord Melody Method MB97343BCD*

Fascination

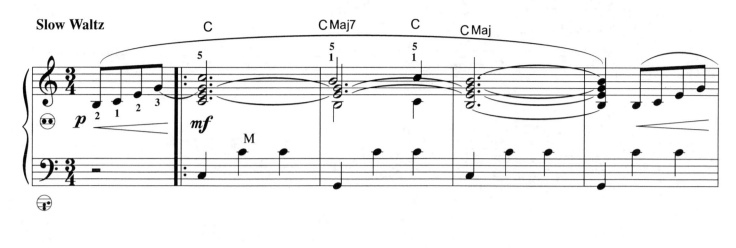

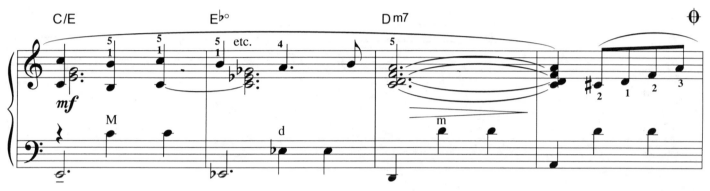

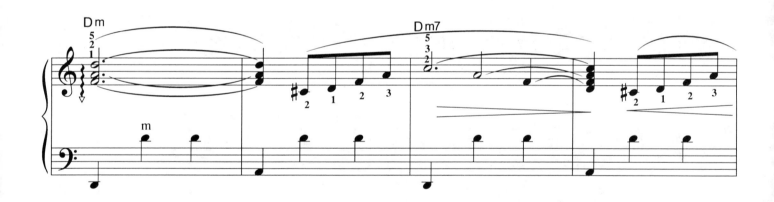

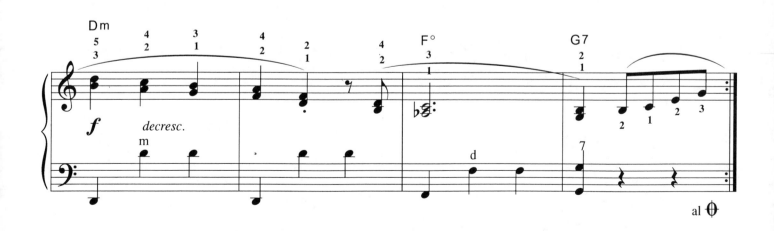

Ja Da

(Use measure 4 for a
repeat if desired)

An Old Time Waltz

NOTE: From this point on the study pieces become progressively complex. Become familiar with each hand alone first.

Try to practice slowly enough to eliminate mistakes.

Do not practice mistakes.

Do not practice from the beginning to the end until thoroughly learned. Practice small sections.

44

Peg O' My Heart

Amazing Grace

Slow Gospel

Chord only style . . . let your bass row finger find location.

legato

a tempo

* Observe all ties

Red River Valley and Home On The Range
a study in intervals, 3rds, 6ths and 2 part writing

Home On The Range

* tenuto, hold full value   ① slide thumb when necessary throughout

Maria, Mari

E. DiCapua
arr. by Gary Dahl

Intermediate
Key of C minor

Key of C Major

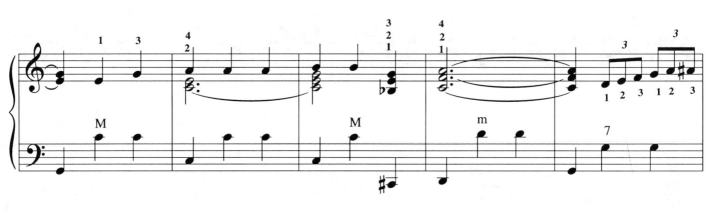

America
a study in larger chords

Be careful with bellows change of direction because the large block chords use more air.

Music by Samuel Smith, 1832

Slowly and Reverently

Molto Expressione

rit.

Repeat as Desired

Marijana

Traditional Croatian

Let Me Call You Sweetheart

slide thumb from B♭ to G

R.H. fingerings: there are many variations... ask your teacher

Mattinata
Morning Serenade

Intermediate

Ruggiero Leoncavallo

59

America the Beautiful
A Patriotic Hymn

Music by Samuel Ward
Words by Katherine Bates

Intermediate

Be bellows careful... this arr. uses more
air because of R.H. block chords.

Legato
smoothly as a slur

Remember: do not change bellows while holding any note.

Change bellows direction when starting a new phrase

rit. last time

cresc.

molto rit.

60

Rockin' the Blues

#19

Gary Dahl

to next strain
2nd time

61

Just a Closer Walk with Thee

Medium Gospel Beat

Same as: ♪♪ ♪♪ rhythm used for gospel, jazz, swing, dixie.
Count: 1 & a 2 & a not as abrupt as ♪. pattern.

63

A Mighty Fortress Is Our God

Martin Luther
arr. by Gary Dahl

J.S. Bach used this theme for a chorale; Mendelssohn used it for Symphony #5, 'The Reformation'

Tango of the Roses

Music by Schreier-Bottero

Moderato

* Use extensive cresc. and dim. throughout.

O Mio Babbino Caro
Gianni Schicchi

Puccini

* ⁶⁄₈ Time: ♪ = 1 count, ♩ = 2 counts, ♩. = 3 counts, 𝅗𝅥. = 6 counts.

Nessun Dorma
Turandot

Andante sostenuto

Puccini

(Leave 2 and 5 in place)

Suggest purchasing a music dictionary

70

Un Bel Di Vedremo
One Fine Day – Madame Butterfly

Andante

Puccini

72

73

Tarantella Napoletana

12th Street Rag

* Slide on upbeat of 2nd count. Slide with thumb and end with the 2nd finger cross over... this is accurate for a long slide.

Come Back to Sorrento

Ernesto di Curtis

85

Optional: add a C minor arpeggio after the last note or an ascending chromatic scale.

Blue Danube Waltz

Johann Strauss

The Moldau

Vltava

Symphonic Poem from the cycle *My Fatherland*

B. Smetana (1824-1884)

Allegro Moderato

Chords held slightly throughout

93

Visit: www.accordions.com/garydahl

For more solo selections visit: www.petosa.com/dahl

Cavaquinho

(Cava - Keen - Yo)

Samba movida

Ernesto Nazareth
arr. by Gary Dahl

97

NOTES

NOTES

NOTES